PRAISE FOR SAMEER KOCHURE'S BOOKS_

A Young Boy And His Best Friend, The Universe. Vol. 1-10.

A soothing read... it instantly puts a smile on your face! :)

- READER REVIEW

Very cute and same time educating book. I recommend it to everyone... if you had a bad day or a good one.

- READER REVIEW

And all of a sudden, the memory of my loved ones flashed back. The story went straight to my heart.

- READER REVIEW

Very nice collection of stories about big questions of life, presented in a very delightful and easy to consume way. I would definitely give it to my teenager kids to read it as well!

- GOODREADS REVIEW

Sameer has distilled the "WISDOM OF THE MASTERS" in just about 100 pages... It is as if the message is for you as you needed it, at this point of time... Please read this book to evolve spiritually. This book will make you happy.

- READER REVIEW

A light insightful read into every human mind. The book connects to the child in everyone and answers the issues faced by every adult. A must have on every kindle for the days when child like wonder is needed the most.

- READER REVIEW

This was a wonderful spiritual story about the friendship between a young boy and the universe. A story about how to think differently than you might at this time and how to appreciate what is around you. It may answer some of your questions, ease your fears or make you look at life differently, no matter what situations arise.

- GOODREADS REVIEW

The Tiny Fireball

A cute, wholesome sci-fi fantasy featuring a star-hopping alien.

"This book is so beautiful..."

- Review on Netgalley

"I would definitely recommend this for fans of Neil Gaiman... and for fans of Life of Pi..."

- Review on Netgalley

"I can't wait to read it again..."

- Review on Netgalley

"A story full of hidden truths and ancient wisdom..."

- Review on Amazon

"Loved the characters and their world...."

- Review on Netgalley

"I enjoyed the story so much..."

- Review on Netgalley

TOUGH SKINS TENDER HEARTS

MENTAL HEALTH & HEALING POETRY-VERSE

SAMEER KOCHURE

B19, Sangam CHS, Sai Baba Road,

Off SV Road, Santacruz West,

Mumbai - 54, India.

author(@)sameerkochure(.)com

Author photo by Ahsan Ali.

Tough Skins, Tender Hearts by Sameer Kochure | First Edition | Paperback

Written and Published by Sameer Kochure.

ISBN 9789334361988

Formatted with Vellum

In its essence, poetry is the subtle alchemy of a sensitive soul.

- LINDA GOODMAN.

CONTENTS_

SOUNDTRACK_

Book Playlist

.

Ever wondered, *'Why can't books have a soundtrack?'* We agree. Go to https://spoti.fi/3q6VYIP or scan the QR code below, and enjoy author curated playlist that compliments this book.

Featured Artist ♫

Use a different music streaming service? Love cool music? Check out this rising indie artist we love.

https://linktr.ee/hridaytalurmusic

To my Aai,
Sunanda Pramod Kochure,
the toughest tender heart
I will ever know.

PROLOGUE_

The mind tells us beautiful stories,

But a man's heart lays bare the truth.

- SAMEER KOCHURE

Welcome to an unveiling, an understanding, an unravelling of the man's heart.

As painlessly as possible, we will rip open a man's ribcage and put the soft, quietly beating muscle under our microscope, in an effort to unlock its mysteries.

What will we find?

Perhaps some hope, some desires, some fears.

A few battle hardened scars, way too personal dreams, wounds yet to heal, maybe a tender moment or two.

Maybe something more?
Let's go and explore.

Love,
Sameer Kochure.
19 - 07 - 2023.

BREAKING_

i tried to write a poem
about men's issues...
there was a fairly short list
of topics to choose...
not because there was
a dearth of troubles they face,
just because
men's issues don't always
make headlines on primetime space.

FATHERHOOD_

big eyes, tiny feet...
    i wonder whether
    they've made a mistake
    and handed me the wrong one
    'cos how could this
    soft little ball of perfection
    come from me,
    one so full of imperfections?

TOUGH SKINS, TENDER HEARTS_

i was born soft and squishy
much like you...
brimming with innocence,
full of toothless wonder...
it's the harsh world out there
that has made me hard out here...
but invest a moment
and look under the hood
and you'll see
a different story emerge...
my skin may be tough,
it may look weathered,
my chest might be hard,
and it could be chiseled,
but deep within,

my heart is still tender...
you may not often see it,
nor may i often show it,
but this tender heart of mine
still feels a bit much,
it still bleeds a bit too much.

MAKING LOVE_

the way you play with my hair
    when i rest my head on your lap
    or the way you hug me
    and fall asleep on the couch
    on our movie nights...
    in my head, i count
    all those times as making love.

IDIOT_

of all the names you give me
and all the things you call me,
the way you smile and say 'idiot'
now that...
that is my favourite.

TEASE_

oh yes we men are strong,
how else would we
be able to survive
the relentless attack all night
of those teasing eyes
from across the bar?

SURVIVE_

i wonder if
i built you up in my memory
all these years...
convinced myself
you deserved someone better...
made you nicer in my mind
than you probably ever were...
more lovely than any human being
could possibly be on this earth...

i wonder if
you built me up
into a monster
in your mind

during the same time
made me meaner, harsher,
angrier than i ever was...
worse than any human being
could possibly be on this earth...

and
i wonder if
we both did it only because,
even after all this time apart,
we just couldn't stop living
in each other's hearts...
and the only way to survive
was to tell ourselves
these lies.

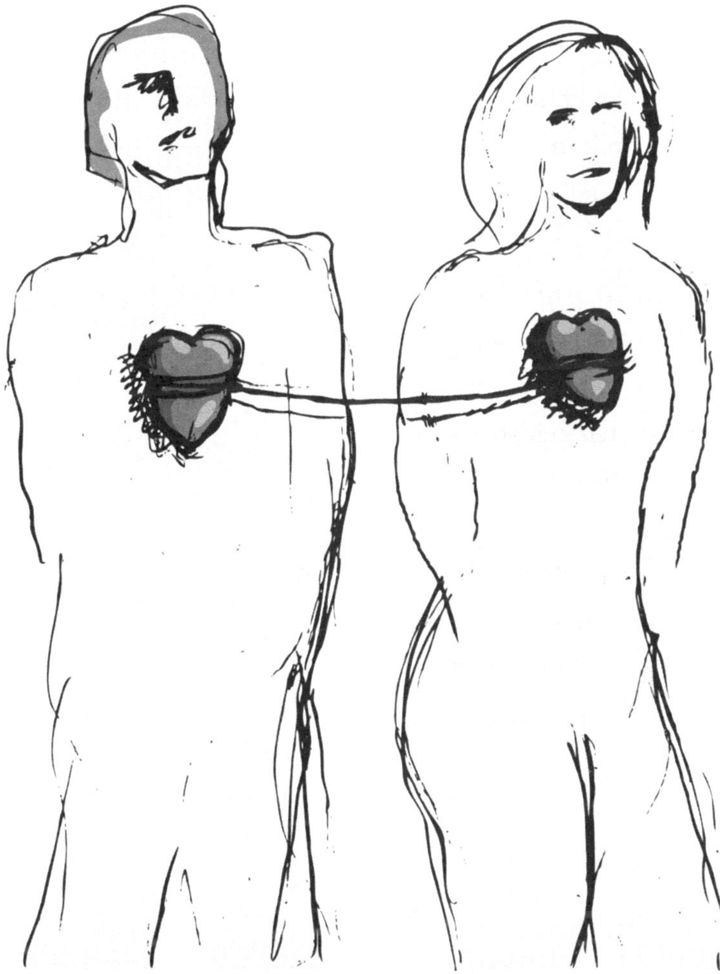

NO FIGHT_

there are nights
when it shows up unannounced
the loneliness and the despair...
i used to be bothered by it,
fight it to sleep...
always, it was a losing battle
now i know better,
now when it shows up,
i am learning to accept it
to let it fill me up
so that i disappear
and i become that loneliness.
when it meets no fight,
nor resistance
it must get bored,

for soon after, it leaves...
perhaps looking for a good fight
someplace else.
whatever shows up in it's place,
i become it next.

COURAGE_

why does the world
teach us men
to hide our inner selves,
lest we come across as weak?
does it not know that
to have a soft heart,
in an exceedingly hard world,
is an act of rebellion,
an act of surprising courage?

BRICKS AND BRIDGES_

wherever i find a hole
i try and fill it
with bucket loads...
with words
in all shapes and sizes
some teeny tiny
and some long and wide
...i never really know
if it is a small ditch
or a valley i'm trying to fill
my hope is
the hole will eventually cease
or at least
i'll have built myself
a little bridge

to take me safely
to the other side...
my words are
the truest bricks i know
and the only gaps
i am trying to fill
lie deep within
my very soul.

CRACK_

i was the dam
you were the crack...
then we met.
now you've disappeared,
and i have nothing left.

YOU KNOW, RIGHT?_

does it ever occur to you
    that i fix those leaky pipes
    and those wobbly tiles
    around the house
    not because
    i love doing those things
    but because i love you?

PERMANENCE_

why do i feel
    they are talking about a stranger
    when they misspell my name?
    why so much importance on a label
    that was only born after i did
    and will leave me as soon as
    i leave this body.

i was there before the label was
    and i'll will be there, in an unknown form,
    after the label is gone,
    so why do i identify and associate
    everything in between to it?

maybe the miseries in life
come by attaching so much importance
to something way more impermanent
than the permanent in me.

DADS AND DAUGHTERS_

it's true,
i will never measure up to your dad...
but i promise
to bring up our daughter such that
she never finds a man
who will measure up to her dad.

VROOM, VROOM!_

yeah, we men love cars.
some of us like them fast
and some of us like
the ones made of legos...
that's just how we roll.

BUILD US UP_

when i spend hours
building, tinkering
and fixing things
around the house,
it's because i know that
you are in my life, building our life,
and it's my way of helping you
build a home for us.

BE A MAN_

well, excuse me!
    i am too busy being me
    to conform to your notion
    of the 'right' way
    of being me.

RATION_

even when the level of hurt is the same,
    why does a man need ration his tears
    while a woman gets no limit on hers?

SONS AND DAUGHTERS_

sometimes i wish
    my father had abused me
    hit me, punched me and
    kicked me in the gut.
    battered me, shattered my bones,
    fractured my skull.
    broken my jaw,
    left me bleeding, hurting, rotting,
    outside my own home,
    at night, in the pouring rain.
    assaulted me so hard,
    with such a degree of violence,
    that even the neighbours
    would be too scared to intervene,
    or call for help.

reduced my existence
to worse than that of a dog,
for even strangers
show the stray a wee bit of care.
sometimes i wish my father
had done these despicable things
to me when i was young...
instead my own child
did them to me
when i was old and worn.

.

my son left me in that state
unable to move, let alone stand and escape.
three sons i had, and a daughter.
when the neighbours called her
she dropped everything,
grabbed her teen daughter's hand,
and caught the first midnight train.
if i am able to tell you my story today,
it's because of this borrowed life of mine
that she came and gave.

WORLDLY AMBITIONS_

no long titles, nor long cars,
    all my worldly ambition
    consists of raising happy kids
    in a loving home not too far.

IN IT TOGETHER_

if only for a moment,
    and only a moment please,
    tell me, would you
    be the stronger one?

UNKNOWN TERRAIN_

forgive me if i stumble and stutter
for i have never really been taught
how to make sense of, nor express,
all that goes on in my heart.

BLEED TO HEAL_

if my words heal you
then i'll happily let my veins
run dry on these pages.

christopher mccandless,
aka alexander supertramp, wrote
'happiness is only real when shared.'
he wrote it with a pen and paper,
but the only reason his words,
and his life, became immortal
is because he lost his life on a grand adventure
into the wild, away from civilisation.
so, i wonder, whether those words of his,
the ones that have doubtlessly

sparked joy for millions were indeed written
by the life force gushing through his veins.
today, decades after he has gone,
his words are still healing me,
and now, healing you too...
that's how, i believe,
his grand adventure continues.

FIRE AND STEEL_

fire in the eyes,
muscles of steel
and a heart that melts
at the sight of kittens...
i am a man
made of contradictions.

SHOES_

why, yes,
i am a man and
i love shoes.
now i could care about
not fitting your stereotype
but then,
i would have less time
for my shoes.

LACK IN ANOTHER_

the first step to falling in love
    is to love your life for what it is,
    and yourself for what you are...
    tides turn, that's life.
    but if you have learnt to find
    love in yourself first,
    you'll never find
    a lack of it in another.

MAKE MY DAY_

yeah,
    a compliment
    makes my day too.

A TIMELESS TALE_

i've loved him
i've depended upon him
i've been embarrassed by him
i've hated him
i've been ashamed of him
i've despised him...
then,
after a long, long,
way too long a time,
i've understood him.
then i've needed him
and then finally
i've loved him again...
that's the story of me
and my dad.

HOW I WISH_

i wish
the world would just pause
when you giggle at something i say,
so i could get drunk on
my favourite sound in the world
a little longer.

BECAUSE OF YOU_

i wish you had my eyes in your eyes
so you could see yourself the way i see you

i wish you had my heart beating in yours
so you could see how all it does, is sing of you

i wish you dreamt my dreams
so you could see how colourful they are

because of you.

SCRAMBLED_

what becomes of the shell
    when one makes an omelette?
    or boils it for precisely 4?
    hardboiled to perfection and
    the shell tossed to oblivion.
    do we worry about the fate of the shell?
    do we cry, wail and mourn its passing?
    then why do pay in tears
    for the ones who seem lost?
    the shell is gone,
    the essence has transformed.
    the shell, the omelette
    and everything else we perceived,
    all are just the vehicles to accomplish
    our missions, and to journey through.

LIVING THE NIGHTMARE_

dreamt me a nightmare last night.
we weren't together.
woke up terrified.
we still weren't together.

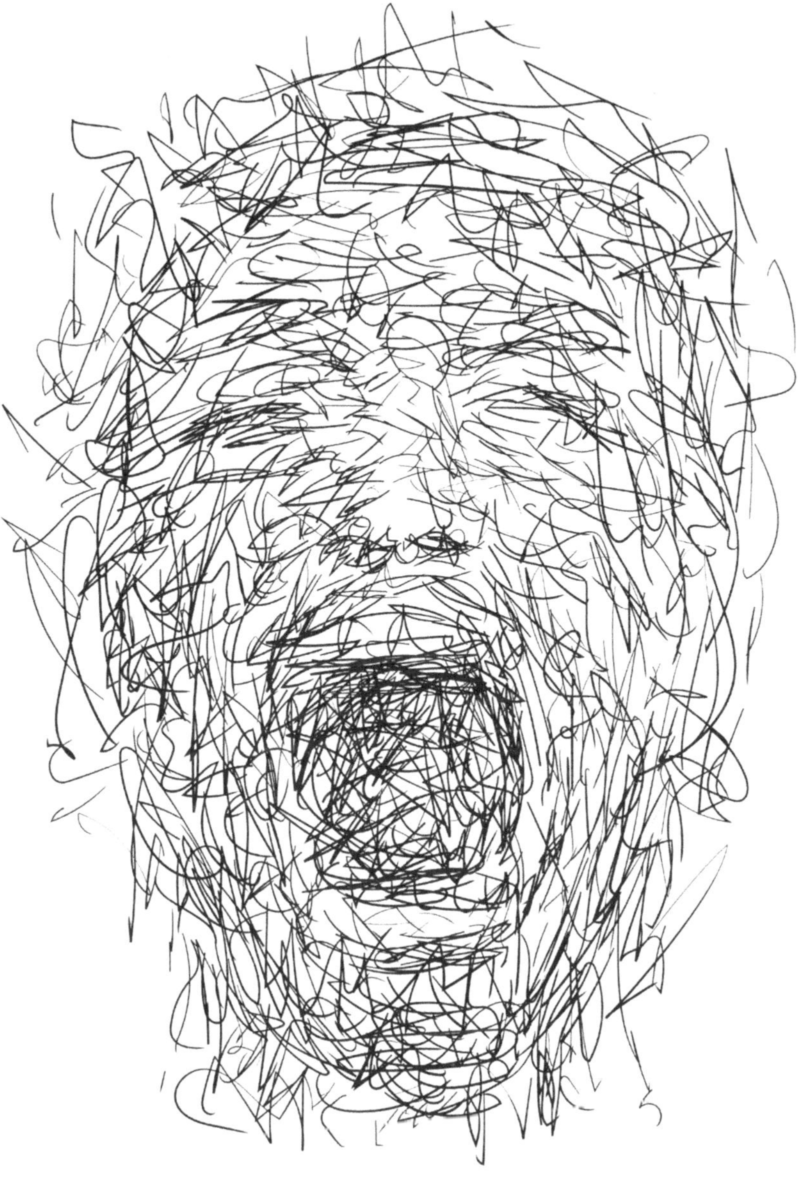

IT'S A MATCH!_

we've invented
a modern antidote
to loneliness and emptiness...
get on a device
swipe left and right
find something you like
tease a bit, flirt a little
rush to gratification...
be self conscious and
feel inadequate all the while
take more than you give
feel the dopamine rush
then leave it all behind
feeling emptier and lonelier
than ever before...

only to repeat the process
soon as you must...
i wonder, would someone
be so kind to tell me,
why did we model
the process of dating
after the act of
streaming porn?

IRON-CLAD_

what a tree lacks
in the movement of its mighty trunk
it makes up for
in the dance of careless abandon
of its leaves and twigs...
just like how
some of the mightiest chests
are carefully constructed
rock-hard armours,
built to protect and shelter
some of the tenderest hearts.

THE MIDNIGHT VISIT_

you sneaked into my dream again tonight
woke me up and
left me turning in my bed since 2.43 am
you wanted to go to a concert together
but shh... no one must know
like the whole relationship
we had so long ago...
it left me feeling so tense
cos i didn't know what to say or do
you grabbed my hand
but i couldn't squeeze it tight like i used to
what am i to do?
you went out and had a whole new life
one whole and complete with
a husband and cute kids

and you still have it going nice and sweet,
at least from the distance it seems
so what are you doing coming here and
leaving me cold sweating past midnight?
what am i do?
what am i to feel?
is this some kind of love?
or is it only grief?

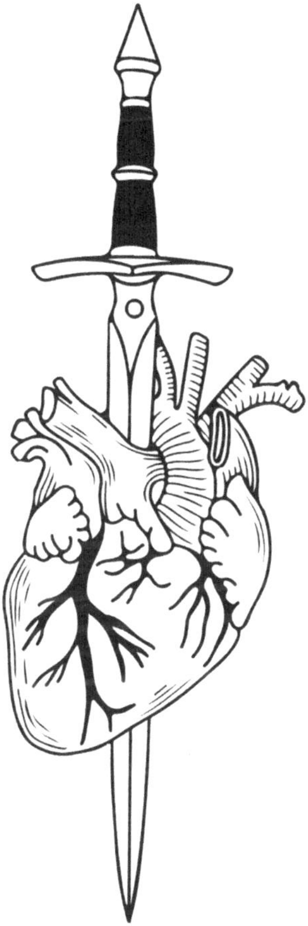

JAPANESE ART FOR THE SOUL_

you are broken,
i am broken.
you are incomplete,
i've never felt complete.
let's gather our gold,
let's meet up someplace,
let's meet up sometime soon.
let's put our gold together,
and mend our broken souls
into one complete whole.
the gold will shine through
the wounds and the cracks
that we have gathered separately
but together we will reattach.

YOU'LL NEVER KNOW_

i wonder if we will meet again,
when we are old and grey...
and you'll wonder what
your life could have been in my arms...
and i will wonder what kind of person
i could have been in yours.

FIVE LETTER WORD_

it took me a long time being angry
to realise the source of my anger
and no, it wasn't the other guy
or some other guy,
or the situation, or the world
that drove me up the wall...
it took a lot of courage
to look within my anger
to study it unafraid
to find its origin
to really understand it...
finally i discovered
'anger' is a 5 letter word
that is commonly misspelt
in truth, it begins with 'g'

and ends with 'rief'
and the only way
to deal with my anger
is not to count to 10
or take a deep breath
but to heal those wounds
that i have long buried
deep inside my chest.

WISDOM GAINED_

i loved you more than i ever loved myself
particularly after you chose to walk out on us.
only today i realised why i have been
so long without experiencing true love
and a meaningful connection...
because i never felt true love
or a meaningful connection
in my own heart, with my own self.
and the only way to crawl out of this mess
is to start adoring my own self,
in my own heart, with my every breath...
the time i may have lost is wisdom gained
and the lovely tomorrow to come
starts here, on this page, today.

ABSOLUTE CHAOS_

i wonder what are you doing
    at this very moment...
    the moment i am thinking of you.
    right here, right now.
    pray tell me, what are you up to?
    besides, of course,
    turning things upside down,
    throwing everything sideways
    burning all maps,
    jamming all gears, derailing all plans,
    causing utter chaos and dysfunction...
    please oh please, do tell,
    what are you doing right now besides
    starting a protest, a movement, a rebellion
    in the deepest recesses of my heart?

DOUBT_

a kind word scares me.
i've been rejected so long
been cheated on so often
been cancelled by the cancel culture
by everyone, and by the world
that even a smiling stranger
automatically throws up my shields
brings down the shutters and
draws out my suspicion.
it's not an ideal way to live,
but it's the only one
that has helped me live.

LANGUISH_

and when we were spent,
and our breaths recovered,
how i loved to gently move
my hand all over your physical self.
exploring, loving, discovering...
every turn was a new wonder
every curve was a ballad,
a sonnet, a novel.
you were all beautiful,
smooth and soft all over.
then i would rest my head
over your chest and listen
to the song of your heart...
it always sang so sweet
a melody of rare, timeless beauty

and of an eternal love...
soon i were to discover
it was all a facade.
underneath the pretty
and the cool and the soft shell,
lay a cold and a calculating heart.
the worst of it was,
the fool that i was,
i still continued pining for
that same ruthless heart.

INSECURITIES - IYKYK_

how big is too big?
how little is too little?
how long is good enough?
ouch!
why is this ruler so cold?

COMPLIANCE_

i step out of my bed
out of my house
wade though the sea
on every street, on every road
fight to park my 'boat'
enter a castle,
a hightower prison,
made of glass and chrome
trade my hours
my sweat, my blood
at times, my dignity even,
for a few, rough-cut pieces
of reluctantly tossed silver...
then, weary in my bones,
i find my way home,

long after the dust has settled,
and i try to convince myself
it is all worth it,
it surely is... if it wasn't,
why would everyone be doing it?
and yet again,
i continue to ignore
the mine of gold
that hides within my soul.

.

no more... no. more.

TETHERED_

not gonna lie
your cute smile, pretty face and sparkling eyes,
that's what caught my attention at the first glance
but the eyes that light up when they meet mine
the heart that makes mine blush
and the soul that sings,
dances and vibes with mine,
now that,
that's what keeps me tethered to you.

BIAS_

picture a hospital emergency room.
three patients are wheeled in.
someone who has been brutally raped at work.
a battered domestic violence survivor.
a college sa victim.
...
how many of them
did you picture as men?
...
just because
we normally don't see, hear, talk,
or even think about it,
doesn't mean it doesn't happen.

THE NEW NORMAL_

shouldn't we normalise
men crying in public already?
it's always the little things.

ABNORMAL_

we feel guilty
we feel deprived
we feel unlucky
we feel unjust
we feel loved
we feel hurt
we feel wonder
we feel grief
we feel repressed
we feel caressed
we feel depressed
we feel mad
we feel glad
we feel sad
we feel nothing

we feel everything
we
are
men
and sometimes,
we need a reminder that
to feel insecure and abnormal
is perfectly fine and normal.
for everyone.
even us.

TYPECAST_

tall, dark and handsome
or
soft, shy and wholesome
rewrite the stereotype.

CONSENT_

consent works both ways too.
please ask.
we will most likely say yes,
even eagerly and happily,
at least, most of the times.
but please ask.
some of us have been
wounded in the past too
and some of those wounds
are barely healed.

PURPOSE_

when you find yourself
surrounded by darkness
with no one
to light a match for you
and no one to point the way out,
just look around in the dark and
reach out with your hands...
there's definitely
someone in there,
another helpless soul,
trapped in the darkness with you...
they are the ones
who you are meant to
light a match for
and point the way out.

ISSUES_

we get headaches too.
some, even real ones.
for the all the same, complicated
and unexplainable reasons
that you do.
it has nothing to do with you.
and everything with
what we are going through.
some issues we love to talk about
some we prefer to overcome on our own.
there's one thing you can do to help though.
understand.
especially when it feels hard to.
we may not acknowledge when you do,

but we will notice.
and we will love you more for it.

ALWAYS HOME_

i was always looking for the one
who will make me feel at home,
the one who will be my home.
however perfect the person,
that idle was always hard to meet.
then i learnt whenever
i feel at home with myself, within myself,
when i welcome my insecurities,
accept my failings and embrace my scars,
wherever i go,
whoever i am with, or however alone,
i am always at home.

NON-NEGOTIABLE_

your head scribbled the terms
"nothing serious."
my head signed the contract.
your heart countersigned as a witness,
while mine was instantly smitten,
never bothered reading the terms.
...
can't blame you now,
you made it clear at the start,
the agreement was final, binding,
and your terms non-negotiable.

A SUMMER SONG_

my heart bled for you
for nearly a decade and some change
wailed and sobbed and claimed unrequited love
that could drive anyone insane
i decided to put the grief to good use
and write a book of love in the honour of you
i started writing
but barely made it into a chapter or two
before the muse ran out
i thought maybe there was no skill in me
to write of a love so great
only when i went deep and took an honest stock
i realised there wasn't
much love in us to write about after all
what i considered our so called 'book of love'

was a mere summer song,
a duet that i continued to sing solo
long after even the following winter was gone...
what i thought would turn out to be
a timeless tomb of love is the only book
i have ever left unwritten...
today i see it as complete though...
a complete success, only because
it remained unfinished, after all.

WHOOSH!_

the brass had a dim sheen,
    like the sun peering through
    an overcast winter sky.
    the two rivets binding
    the brass to the leather
    had the same sheen, albeit
    a bit smaller, like smaller suns.
    the leather that made the body
    came in the colour of tobacco,
    smelt the same too,
    result of calloused hands
    being tucked in it after
    rolling uneven, thick cigarettes.
    the width of the leather
    was a healthy 1 and 3/4 of an inch,

one that required jeans loops
that only came on cowboy cuts those days.
the craftsmanship was impeccable,
handmade by hands that loved the work.
the leather was well-oiled,
for durability and aesthetic reasons.
it was a fine item made to last,
made to outlast normal wear and tear,
made to withstand normal abuse and lack of care.
the leather was thick too,
when wrapped around the fist
it made a sizeable punch,
not quite as big as a boxer's glove,
but just as strong on impact, maybe more.
definitely more.
the leather made
a lovely whooshing sound as well
when it whipped through the air
and stuck my back...
or often, as it stuck my mum's.
dad had issues.
and a mighty fine belt.

RESPONSIBILITY_

there's a certain 'lost and found'
it's the biggest in town,
all the items laying there unclaimed
are stacked-up sky high,
that pile is easily a million mile wide...
the things that make up this pile
are all shapes and size,
teeny tiny to big and grave...
all these items go by
a common name - 'mistakes'.
abandoned and orphaned by fools
revered as treasures by the wise few...
such is the fate of these
poor little precious things,
the mistakes that no one claimed.

ABRACADABRA!_

the apple fell on a young thinker's head,
and the law of the universe he discovered...
once upon a time, way back when,
he ate an apple that was a full meal
for his tiny stomach
the remains and the pit
he placed in a hole in his backyard,
covered it with soil
and cast a magic spell upon it
'abracadabra!' was the most potent one
he could conjure.
many moons rose and many moons waned
he grew up practical and worldly-wise
shunned magic and all such vice.
then one fine day,

now grown into a big and important man
with all grown up worries and big problems,
he stepped in to his garden
looking for a moment of respite,
that's when the apple landed
square on his head with aplomb...
he looked up at all the juicy fruits
hanging above his head,
smiled, took a big, sweet bite and
started believing in magic once again.

CONTENTMENT_

no riches as rich as contentment
no burden heavy when expressed
no happiness lasting unless shared
no joy bigger than giving
no helping hand that weighs less than gold
no results without a cause
no limits that can't be broken
no fate that can't be rewritten
no dream, failure or success final
no love true until without condition.

TWIN FLAMES_

what a fool i was
i thought we were in love
we weren't, we were in pain
now that we are no longer together
we are in love once again
irrationally, utterly,
deliriously in love with each other
across this cosmos,
as far as the light reaches,
as far as our thoughts travel,
as long as hope lives,
we will be in love...
and until the end of everything,
in love we will remain.

WITH YOU_

i felt
unwanted.
unheard.
unseen.
uncertain.
undone.
unfulfilled.
unimportant.
unsafe.
unstable.
unworthy.
unloved.
unnecessary.

then,
you came around.
and,

i felt
understood.
unafraid.
uncomplicated.
unbroken.
undamaged.
uncommon.
unceasing.
undivided.
unimpeded.
unstoppable.
unconditional.
unfettered.

that's my complicated way
of telling you that now
all the good things in my life
begin with you.

COLLIDE_

you could be anywhere.
around the corner,
across the galaxy.
a moment or
a million lifetimes away.
you could be in the car
next to me at the traffic stop,
or getting a green light
to go on a mission to mars.
sometimes i feel
this universe is far too big
far too fickle, far too wide...
a place where hearts
meant to meet
take forever to collide.

THE PERFECT DUET_

i'll be the shoulder you lean on
you be the lap i rest my head on
together, we will sail through life
like a sweet summer song.

THE END OF TIME_

i love the me
i am becoming when i am with you,
perhaps this is the ultimate test
to know if our love is true
for you may change tomorrow
that's how life works,
every morning a new sun rises,
and i won't be able to
stop you from changing,
nor demand that you don't,
no amount of begging, pleading or wishing
can stop you from being the truest you...
but if i take care of loving me
when i am with you

then i think we will make it just fine,
and they will sing stories of our love
till the end of time.

BUZZZ!_

a single drop of rain
  is 5 times the size of an average mosquito...
  when it pours, it lashes down hard
  on this sibling of a certain transylvanian count
  if the drop hits the tiny limbs or the wings,
  it veers and wobbles the mosquito
  the way a nasty turbulence
  jerks and jolts an aircraft
  if the raindrop lands square on the jaw,
  and therefore smack in the middle
  of the body of the mosquito,
  the sheer weight and volume of it
  sends the mosquito into a tailspin,
  and causes it to rapidly lose its altitude
  but the exoskeleton

of this little blood guzzler
is surprisingly strong
made to withstand
countless raindrops just as strong
shadowy clouds may gather,
it may thunder and pour,
but the humble little mosquito
keeps flying on, come rain or hailstorm
the odds only seem unsurmountable
when we pause to consider them
perhaps we ought to learn a thing or two
from our mate, the pesky little flying fellow,
and when we find ourselves facing similar odds
when the clouds gather overhead
cut out our light, '*boo*' us and intimidate...
when it all comes crashing down,
let us spread our own wings and keep flying on,
trusting that we will be alright
for the power that powers
the wings of the tiny mosquito
flows through our veins too...
and if a humble mosquito can do it,
why can't me and you?

PDA_

leaning into one another,
challenging physics,
trying to merge into one...
whispering a decibel under audible,
having complete conversations
silently with their eyes...
getting drunk on each other's smiles...
ravenously filling up on each other by sight,
sweet hungers unsatisfied...
true lovers in public are an absolute delight.

KINDLING_

there are only two in our marriage
me and you,
alive, healthy and reasonably well,
but there's a third, dead as stone,
and that's our bedroom.
agreed,
we are no longer as young,
and our bodies are squishy
where they were once firm
but still,
they belong to us, they are our own...
as are our dreams,
our minds and our thoughts,
the same things in each other we fell for...
i believe, my love,

the embers still burn, and
with a little kindling, gathered together,
the fires will, once again, awaken.
we've built our whole lives together
now let's rebuild our bedroom,
our love, our bond forever.

EQUILIBRIUM_

shade, cleanse, hydrate.
while i was learning to love myself
from everything in creation...
while i was learning to realise that
everything was made for me...
while i was learning that
i was made for everything and
i belonged to creation...
somewhere in between
nourishing my spirit and
merging with the spirit of the eternal,
i learned to love my soul,
as i was taught to love my skin...
shade and protect from the evils

that swirl around, ready to pounce...
cleanse and purify my mind,
free it from craving and aversion...
and hydrate my soul on the pure ecstasy
of the ultimate equilibrium.

UNWELL_

went to the doc
got myself checked
did all the tests
the sonograms, the x-rays,
th ecgs, the ultrasounds,
the ct scans, even the mri...
the investigations were all a failure.
the veins and the ventricles,
the nerves and the tissues,
all looked like a crowded mess,
yet, were as fit as they ever were
and ever could be...
what was missing
was a teeny tiny switch,

the one that i could flick off
and stop the earnest craving
deep within my heart
for all that is, was, and ever will be,
you.

POOF!_

this thing,
the thing between us,
if it is real
how can it just disappear?
and if it disappeared so readily,
was it ever real?

ETERNAL_

real love stories
don't have a last chapter,
the final scene,
a last goodbye,
fade to black,
or the words 'the end' printed
in a beautiful calligraphic flourish.
the real love stories
pick up where they left off
on another page
in another dimension
in a new era
in new skins
in a new world.

the suns set,
the shadows fade,
the forms change...
the energy remains.

SURVIVOR_

the word 'rape' has no gender.
nor does the word 'victim'.
so why the bias when
those two words are put together?
experts believe that almost
10% of rape victims are men
and
sexual assaults on men are under-reported.
they say, the victims fear being ridiculed
and are afraid
their plight won't be taken seriously,
even by their friends and inner circle.
'trauma' has no gender. 'no' has no gender.
neither does compassion.
a survivor is a survivor.

POCKETFUL_

back when i was a kid in short droopy pants,
my shorts drooped lower one day cos
i had a handful of rainbow marbles in my pockets
all the kids in the playground who saw them
wanted to be my friend that day
they wanted me to trade my marbles
for the sticks and
stones they had, even some hay...
some asked, some cajoled
and some plainly begged me
to let them play with my marbles that day...
it was a fun day i spent at the park,
unlike many before
where not one kid had come close,
less still, ask me

to join their group, or their game...
it was not long before my pockets tore
from the burdens they bore,
and all the marbles fell to the floor...
my new friends scattered after them
faster than they had gathered around me...
they picked and clutched all the marbles
that they could snatch from the ground...
'finders keepers!' was their cry and shout
as they ran away with their shiny new treasures,
claiming it theirs what was mine a wink before...
i was frozen, glued to the spot,
and now also all alone, as all were gone...
i wondered if all they wanted
were the marbles i brought
was a true friend so hard to be sought?
now that i am grown,
the playground, the kids and the marbles,
all look different and go by different names,
but
the original question has remained unchanged.

OWN IT._

tall. dark. handsome.
rugged. brooding. gruff.
dad-bod. dad jokes. dad.
short. stout. shy.
mysterious. deep. quiet.
fun. flabby. funny.
vegan. ripped. contradiction.
hurt. tender. healing.
___. ___. ___.
the world's definition
of what is attractive is incomplete.
add what you are.
own. what. you. are.

HOME_

i wish i had a remote
with only one button
i would press it
and the city would go mute
all the electric lights would go out
and my home would be lit by the stars...
then i think
i already have that remote
it looks like my two feet
if the starlight and the quiet
can't reach me where i live,
i'll let my feet take me
to where they live...
after all, they too are my kin,
and that too, is my home.

THE BRO CODE_

it's a sacred bond
that binds one man to the other,
two brothers from different mothers...
but what does it really mean?
it means i will be there for you, dude.
need a drinking partner, call on me.
need someone to vent about your job,
your girl or about anything at all,
i am there mate.
need someone to move,
i will grab a 6 pack on the way over,
and don't you forget, the pizza is on you!
need someone to take the fall
to make you look cool in front of the girl
you are trying to impress in the bar?

oh man, the things i do for you...
need someone
to cover up for your little white lies,
sure, no questions asked, no judgements passed.
doing something wrong,
straying off the righteous path?
i will be there to whack you straight and
get you back on the right track.
i will challenge you at the beer pong,
and accompany you to the aa meets,
if things go too far...
i would go to the ends of earth for you
fight the dragons, rescue your princess with you.
i will bail you out of every tight spot,
lift you up if it gets too dark...
i will do what it takes for you, my friend,
knowing fully well,
if our roles are reversed, you will do the same.

CRUMBLING_

write down the names of six men
that are close to your heart.
just do it, don't cheat.
trust the process.
write first, then read further.
1. ________
2. ________
3. ________
4. ________
5. ________
6. ________
chances are one of them has faced
absolute horror that's vile and unimaginable.
one in six.
that's the number of men who have

faced some form of sexual abuse in their lives.

...

when it is just a statistic;
it is just a number, cold and impersonal.
but when you put names against the numbers;
when you realise it could be your favourite uncle,
best mate or someone even closer,
you realise the magnitude of the problem.
the world can be harsher on some.
they may be fighting their battles silently
and keeping their scars hidden.
so, don't ration your compassion only
for the ones who look weak.
a mighty mountain maybe crumbling inside.
your kindness might just be the thing
that it needs it to hold on a little longer,
to keep it together... and heal.

NEVER ALONE_

we could bump into each other outside a café,
juggling our turmeric lattés and laptop bags,
apologise, then smile awkwardly
and secretly wonder
if we are the lead pair in a rom-com...
we could meet at a party
or a corporate workshop
become lovers, or cordial mates
or just a solid, dependable friend...
the one who helps you repair your electric bbq
or complains about helping you move
even as he insists on grabbing
the heavier end of the almirah...
we could pull pranks on each other,
overshare, banter and keep our secrets

you could know me inside out
be best of a friend, a lover, a spouse or a child
but you could still go
a lifetime without knowing about
the demons i battle in my mind and soul...
you may never know about
how difficult it is at times for me
to just drag my body
from the bed into the shower...
or look at myself in the mirror...
to share an acceptable relationship
with good food...
or how dark skies sometimes get
over my head on a beautiful summer day...
i could trust you with my life,
make you my emergency contact
but i could still guard,
hide and protect my fears from you...
you would be right to feel cross
when you first find out
but please understand my dear lover,
friend, or kin of blood,
i'm not guarding my fears, no, no,
i'm protecting you from them...
just because they got me,
doesn't mean i will let them get to you too...

i hope, maybe,
someday i'll be able to sit you down
and tell you what my mind is often up to,
but it is just so hard to explain,
they are no words that reflect what it feels like
when your own throat
refuses to let the air through...
or how a full plate of good food
in front of you
feeds the monster of unworthiness inside you...
there are battles i must fight alone,
storms i must sail through alone,
don't hold it against me please...
but know that while i suffer alone,
with you in my life, i never feel alone.

SA RE GA MA..._

i love

going on long walks
when the sounds of city
start fading
i can hear the universe singing.

READY_

i plan, plot and chart precisely my course,
then just go with the flow...
live with my heart on my sleeve,
and my hand on my sword.

MAGIC!_

the more i work with love
    the more money i make
    the more i live with love
    the more everything just works.

DON'T_

don't cry.
don't be afraid.
don't you dare!
don't you care?
don't be a creep.
don't be a wimp.
don't bother.
don't. just don't.
don't tell me what to do.
i'll make my own mistakes.
i'll learn my own don'ts.

PURPOSE_

our true purpose
    hides within
    what we think is
    our true purpose.

RESPECT_

i was told
all i had to do was grow up...
the sniggering, the constant picking,
making fun of me behind my back,
the snide remarks to my face...
all would stop,
i was told...
just a couple of years,
the school will be through and
these things won't bother you...
then i was told the same
when it came to the higher grades
the patterns played all over again
just a few more years, i was told yet again
soon you'll be out of here and at a job...

hold on, stay stronger, a little longer...
then came work
new place, new environment, new groups
the pattern still, somehow followed me through...
i was once again told
'let it be... put your head down and carry on...'
then i questioned the voice and
realised it was no one else's but my own...
it kept telling me to suffer in silence and endure...
but all this while, it had been a choice
to listen to it... to just take it...
the environment was not a choice,
but to act powerless had been my own choice...
finally i gathered my courage and spoke up
my hands were shaking,
my soul quivered inside,
it had never learnt to stand up for itself yet...
but speaking up one time is all it took,
the message was heard and
in an instant my world changed
all the bullies disappeared, as did my shame...
now i live in a new world,
same place, same people, same environment,
but now, there's a mutual respect...
respect which came from the outside,
when i first gave it to myself.

LET GO_

what i run after, runs from me.
    what i try to run from, blocks my path.
    when i give up this mindless running,
    i get what i want.

THE BLANK CHEQUE_

i signed a blank cheque,
agreed to the conditions without
understanding the terms...
when the high wore off,
when my vision cleared,
by the time my senses returned,
by the time i tried to renegotiate
it was far too late...
what started as fun
ended the same for you
but for me it became
something more, much more,
something that can have no end.

SUCCESS_

there are days
when i wake up and
feel like a complete failure.
i feel lost, like
there is no point to it all...
there are days i feel
no matter what i do,
what i desire the most
keeps running away from me
coast to coast...
there are days
when i wake up and
feel like a complete failure.
...
then i go to work.

so that
for that one day,
when i am
fighting, striving and
bleeding to get ahead...
for that one day
i am not a failure.
that day, i am
a success in progress.

UNBROKEN_

who is the weaker sex?
4 out of 5 suicides are men.
so, who really is the weaker sex?
perhaps, there is no right answer
to that question.
the question itself is flawed,
unnecessary, divisive.
the right question,
the only one that matters,
is how do we heal everyone
who feels so lost,
so vulnerable, so broken?
how do we make all of us
unbroken?

KIND_

humankind.
it's part of our identity.
to be human is to be kind.
what do we really achieve on this earth,
what do we gain,
if we won't show kindness to the ones in pain?
whether be it to our family, friends or foes...
or our own selves?

CHASM_

there was a time i had a friend
some would call us
the best kind that ever came...
we would pull each other's leg
share banter, beer and non-sense
we were there for each other
when the going was rough,
the days be bright, dark or dull...
then something happened
a wedge between us grew to be a chasm
something silly and stupid,
not worth a mention...
yet it festered and turned to poison
sad as it may, sometimes these things happen
there seems no coming back now,

no point looking back now,
too much has happened,
the bridge has been broken...
now they look at us and say
'there go two strangers
who were once the best of mates.'

EXECUTIVE ORDERS_

stepping into a palace
    you better be cautious!
    many a kings
    collected heads of those
    whose tongues were loose,
    whose eyes strayed,
    or gestures betrayed...
    the kings and queens may be gone
    but the royal courts still remain,
    in prestigious corners,
    on high floors
    ensconced in glass and chrome.
    ...
    in the royal shadows
    justice can still be found,

advances can still be made,
the rewards still remain to be won,
even the throne is never out of bound,
provided you can keep
your integrity, your dignity,
and hang on to your dear head.

HEADS UP_

want to tumble and fall?
    then look back, young man.
    want to move ahead?
    then know there's nothing behind,
    not even your past.

GIVE TO KEEP_

if i had a million
    but spent not a buck,
    did i really have any?
    if i loved everyone
    but showed it to none,
    then did i really love?
    if i was happy beyond measure
    but never shared it with a soul
    was my happiness ever real?
    if i could give, and give some more,
    but chose never to do so,
    did i really live?

THE MOUNTAIN_

you can run after the wind
and never catch it
you can chase the clouds,
and they'll keep running away
you can wish and pray for rain
as many do,
and you'll meet empty skies,
like many do too...
but if you become a mountain
quiet and still
firm and unmoving
fixed in your resolve
then the wind will come
and play with you
the sun will shine on you

the clouds will stop by
and rain on you,
cover you with snow too...
guess the mountain
is silently telling us that
everything comes when you
become still and allow it to.

LOOK OUT_

the sun is setting behind me
    as i walk alone, quietly in the park...
    with my head hung low, i gently tiptoe
    now i may look it,
    but no, i am not depressed...
    why, thank you for your concern!
    it's just that
    i have tiny friends down there,
    most of them are
    marching in a disciplined line,
    others are straying for a while...
    some curious, some foraging, some scavenging,
    others still carrying home a seed, a small twig
    or a tiny treasure that's a bread crumb...
    it's them i am looking out for,

them i am trying not to crush...
my tiny friends, my planet mates...
this world is big enough for all of us,
and look out for one another
we all must.

A TABLE FOR TWO_

a table for two.
a sweet little cafe.
not too casual, not too dressy,
just about right
for a first date found on an app
for the ones who have never met,
but have exchanged a few lively chats...
i select a table that's cozy and private,
not the best one in the house though,
don't want to seem too eager...
i thought i'll bring a flower
then thought otherwise,
reasons the same as the seating choice.
didn't come empty handed though,
no sir, not me,

i have brought some jokes,
a patient pair of ears and my best smile.
the clock is ticking, wonder if you are running
a tad longer than fashionably late.
been sipping slowly from a water bottle,
didn't want to order without you,
but now the staff is giving me the eye, what to do?
fine, let me order something, just to
keep them at bay,
i was trying not to be rude
and wait to order with you,
but even a small business has salaries to pay...
so for now, a medium mocha would do...
tick-tock, sip-tock, tick-tock, sip-tock...
my coffee's gone cold,
the minutes are now nearer an hour.
there's a new feeling stirring in my heart.
'that's what you get for trusting strangers
with filters on their face,' it says,
and tops it off with a dash of salt,
'...so this is what being unwanted feels like.'
no one knows it as i walk back home
but i feel everyone sees it on my face,
'there goes the poor chap...'
their gaze seems to say,
'...the poor chap that no one wants to date.'

AUTHOR'S NOTE_

Dear Reader,

I hope you enjoyed this book. I wrote it because there's an abundance of poetry books written about women, only a few about men.

This book is written in the same vein as my previous book 'Made of Flowers and Steel', which celebrates the inner grit and moral fortitude of women.

I have written a lot of poems in both these books in first person. It is nothing more than a creative choice, as I believe it makes the poems powerful and relatable.

A lot of them are based on true stories, they are just not my own true stories. Extensive research has helped me discover and tell these stories.

People going through beautiful or traumatic experiences may not always have the desire, or the inclination, to put them down in words which can heal all of us. So I choose to do that while taking care to respect their privacy and to treat their experience with dignity. Wherever I may have failed, the responsibility lies with me alone.

Few experiences are my own, of course. I believe every book, in part, is an autobiography.

It's impossible for the artist not to insert themselves into their art, that's what makes each piece unique.

I would also like to mention that my spiritual practices inform my art. I primarily circle between three forms of meditation, the Silva method, Vipassana and Brahmavidya (aka Mentalphysics). I recommend them all.

Now, stay tuned for a brief glimpse of 'Made of Flowers and Steel'.

Love,

Sameer Kochure.

19 - 07 - 2023.

Welcome to a poetry collection that celebrates the strength behind the beauty that is a woman.

Inspired by stories of real women, **this collection of 100 poems honours the raw grit and the moral fortitude that exists in all**

women. Sometimes that power is inherent, sometimes it needs to be invoked, but it is always there.

Page after page, you'll discover a newfound love and respect for yourself, and for all the women in your life.

Written by Sameer Kochure, the author of the much adored book series *'A Young Boy and His Best Friend, The Universe,'* and *'Wrong. - An inspirational poetry collection,'* this is an easy to read, yet strikingly powerful work of art.

This is NOT a regular book of poems on love, heartbreak or feminism. **It's a salute to the moral strength it takes to be a woman** in today's world. The steel beneath the flowers.

An empowering and a comfort read for all the thinking, feeling women around the world, and for everyone who loves them.

100 Poems | 1 Unmissable Collection

ARE YOU A GENEROUS READER?_

If you've enjoyed this book, please write a review for it on any two of your favourite online bookstores. That could be any online store where you buy your books. Sites like Goodreads are alright, but most readers discover new books at the point of sale, so you are really helping independent authors like me by publishing your reviews on online bookstores. Moreover, reviews are for readers, plus they have a habit of coming back. You help some stranger discover a book you loved, and out there, right now, there's some kind stranger penning a review for a book you will soon discover and love. Keep the cycle of goodness going, be a generous reader. :)

ALSO BY SAMEER KOCHURE_

The Tiny Fireball

A cute, sci-fi fantasy featuring star-crossed lovers.

* * *

Made of Flowers and Steel

A poetry collection that celebrates the raw grit and inner strength of women.

* * *

Tough Skins, Tender Hearts

Poems about men, for everyone who loves them.

* * *

A Young Boy And His Best Friend, The Universe.

A heartwarming, comfort-read fable. Read all 10 Volumes.

* * *

WHOLESOME CHILDREN'S BOOKS

Dude, you are going to poop!

(Body positivity)

My dear Princess, you are going to fart!

(Body positivity)

Look up at the wonders, kiddo!

(Digital screen detox)

Where do they go...

(Separation anxiety)

When mamma and dadda go mad...

(Arguing adults)

Bullies are like balloons...

(Coping with bullying)

* * *

By the time you are reading this, I may have new books out.
Visit the author site to see the complete list of my books.

www.SameerKochure.com

Book Playlist

Ever wondered, *'Why can't books have a soundtrack?'* We agree. Go to https://spoti.fi/3q6VYIP or scan the QR code below, and enjoy author curated playlist that compliments this book.

Featured Artist ♫

Use a different music streaming service? Love cool music? Check out this rising indie artist we love.

https://linktr.ee/hridaytalurmusic

LIBRARIES_

I love libraries, so I've made all my titles available through most of the libraries worldwide.

In case, you don't find any of my books at your library, just fill out a simple book request form, and they will procure them for you.

Libraries are awesome that way. So, show them some love as well.

ACKNOWLEDGMENTS_

My parents Sunanda & Pramod Kochure, who gave us, their children, everything.

My sister and family, Dr. Monica, Dr. Narahari and Hriday Talur. My aunt and uncle who are more of our second parents, Viju maushi, Tayade uncle. Pinks, Sam, Gau, Ishaan and Khrisha. Jośe Silva, Dr Bimol Rakshit, Burt Goldman and Hemil Shah. Ding Le Mei, SN Goenkaji and Gautama, the Buddha. Hemant Moghe, Mandeep Anand and Vinay Rathod. Ayn Rand and Rahul Bose. Tejal Mamaniya, Mehboob Peerbhai and all spiritual masters who guide me on my path.

I give thanks, I give thanks, I give thanks.

LOVED THE BOOK?_

Your review may help more readers discover this little adventure. So, if you enjoyed reading it, would it be super-inconvenient to leave a quick 5 star review?

ABOUT THE AUTHOR_

Author photo by Ahsan Ali

Sameer Kochure was born in India during the darkest part of the night. Probably explains why he is such a self-proclaimed dreamer. He has lived in 6 cities and 3 countries since. He has also clocked in 12 years as a Creative Director in some of the biggest advertising agencies across Asia Pacific. He lives in Dubai, but claims that anywhere he travels, he feels he is home.

Use the code '**FRB-RDR-15**' to **SAVE 15%** on any book when you get it from the official author website:

www.SameerKochure.com

Subscribe to the author's email list:

www.sameerkochure.substack.com

GRATITUDE_

Thanks for reading.

You are awesome.

9 789334 361988

Printed at Repro India Ltd.